Rock On! A Look at Geology

Super Soils

Christine Petersen
ABDO Publishing Company

visit us at
www.abdopublishing.com

Published by ABDO Publishing Company, 8000 West 78th Street, Edina, Minnesota 55439.
Copyright © 2010 by Abdo Consulting Group, Inc. International copyrights reserved in all countries.
No part of this book may be reproduced in any form without written permission from the publisher.
The Checkerboard Library™ is a trademark and logo of ABDO Publishing Company.

Printed in the United States of America, North Mankato, Minnesota.
092009
012010

 PRINTED ON RECYCLED PAPER

Cover Photo: iStockphoto
Interior Photos: Alamy pp. 11, 14, 16; Getty Images pp. 22, 23, 29; iStockphoto pp. 1, 4, 5, 7, 13, 15,
    17, 20–21, 26–27, 27, 29; Peter Arnold pp. 13, 19; Photo Researchers p. 25;
    U.S. Department of Agriculture p. 19

Series Coordinator: Megan M. Gunderson
Editors: Megan M. Gunderson, BreAnn Rumsch
Art Direction & Cover Design: Neil Klinepier

Library of Congress Cataloging-in-Publication Data

Petersen, Christine.
  Super soils / Christine Petersen.
      p. cm. -- (Rock on! a look at geology)
  Includes index.
  ISBN 978-1-60453-747-5
  1. Soils--Juvenile literature. I. Title.
  S591.3.P464 2010
  631.4--dc22
                              2009033009

Contents

Darwin's Field 4

A Closer Look 6

Getting Your Hands Dirty 10

Cracking Up 12

Getting Carried Away 14

The Circle of Life 16

Land and Climate 18

A World of Soils 20

Looking Below the Surface 22

The Best Soil Around 24

Living with Soil 26

Standing Strong 28

Glossary 30

Saying It 31

Web Sites 31

Index 32

Darwin's Field

In 1871, a trench was dug across a field near Charles Darwin's house. This may seem like ordinary farmwork. But, Darwin was one of the world's most famous scientists. The field was part of an experiment!

This story begins in the 1830s, when Darwin became interested in soil. Over the years, Darwin looked at numerous fields in England. He paid special attention to those left unplanted for many years.

At first, their surfaces were scattered with a layer of rocks and other objects. Over time, the objects appeared to sink into the ground. They still formed a layer. But, it was now farther under the surface! And, it was covered with a dark substance.

Charles Darwin

Darwin looked closely at this black stuff. He recognized that it was made from earthworm **castings**. There were lots of worms in English soil. But could earthworms make enough castings to cover whole farm fields?

In December 1842, pieces of chalk had been spread across that field near Darwin's house. By 1871, all of the chalk had disappeared. After the trench was dug, Darwin saw where the chalk had gone. It was buried seven inches (18 cm) down. New castings were piled on top of it. Darwin's idea was correct. Earthworms help form soil's upper layer!

Earthworms are small, but they move a lot of soil. Scientists estimate they can turn over one inch (3 cm) of all the soil covering Earth in just ten years!

A Closer Look

Earthworms help soil form. But what is soil made of? Unlike Darwin, you don't have to wait 30 years to take a peek into the soil! Ask an adult to help you find a safe place to dig. A nearby garden or yard will work well. Fill a jar with some soil. Be careful not to harm anything living in the soil.

Find a table where you can work. Cover it with newspaper or plastic. Then, spread a handful of soil over the surface. Look closely. Roll the soil between your fingers. Hold it up to your nose. What do you see, feel, and smell?

Scientists know that soil has four main ingredients. These are **organic** matter, **minerals**, water, and air. Much of the organic matter is humus. It comes from decayed plants and animals.

It may be hard to spot water or air in your sample. Yet in the ground, air fills spaces between bits of humus and minerals. Water flows into the spaces after a rain shower. Tiny water droplets cling to soil so plants have something to drink.

Minerals and organic matter affect how soil looks and feels.

Explore Your Soil!

What You'll Need

- **Soil**
- **Jar with lid**
- **Water**
- **Paper towels or newspaper**
- **Spoon**

What You'll Do

1. Ask an adult for permission to dig up soil from a nearby yard.

2. Fill your jar halfway with the soil. Add water until the jar is nearly full.

3. Put on the jar's lid. Make sure it's on tight!

4. Shake the jar for about 30 seconds. The soil and water should be all mixed up.

5. Let the jar sit overnight. The soil will settle and start forming layers.

6. Check out those layers! Larger particles settle at the bottom, and finer particles settle at the top. What layer is thickest in your sample?

7. Do you want to explore these layers further? Spread out paper towels or newspaper on your work surface. Open up the jar and spoon out anything floating at the top. Carefully pour out the water. Then, spoon out each layer of soil. Look at them closely. Rub the soil from each layer between your fingers. Is it smooth like clay or rough like sand?

2

3

4

5

Getting Your Hands Dirty

After that soil experiment, your hands will probably be dirty. Soil may be stuck under your fingernails and in the lines of your palms. But, you don't have to touch soil to get dirty.

Dirt is everywhere! Walk around in your bare feet. Play outside on a summer day. Run your finger over the floor beneath your bed. Then take a look at your skin. There it is, dirt!

Dirt and soil can both create a mess. Sometimes, they even look the same. Yet dirt and soil are quite different. Put simply, dirt makes people and objects unclean. Dirt is something you want to wash off. Soil is something we do not want to get rid of. In fact, we depend on it!

Soil is a thin layer that covers much of Earth's land. It can even be found under shallow water. Soil builds up where **minerals** and humus collect. Where soil forms, plants can grow. They depend on soil for food and water. We depend on plants for the oxygen we breathe and the food we eat. In these ways, soil is an important **natural resource**.

A scientist who studies soil is called a pedologist.

Cracking Up

It may seem like Darwin's earthworms moved a large amount of soil in a short time. Yet soils can take hundreds or thousands of years to develop. Five main factors lead to soil formation. These are parent material, plants and animals, land surface features, climate, and time.

Soils start forming from parent material. This is made from broken-down rocks. Rocks are made of **minerals**. So, they provide one of the four main ingredients of soil.

Much parent material is the result of **weathering**. Water, wind, and plants all cause weathering. During a storm, water may seep into cracks in rocks. If temperatures turn cold, the water freezes. Ice takes up more space than water. So, it pushes against the rock. Small cracks grow larger until the rock finally splits. Water can also **dissolve** certain minerals in rock.

Although wind cannot be seen, it carries small particles. These act like sandpaper. They crash into rock and slowly wear away its surface. Even plants can cause rocks to weather. They often grow into cracks in rocks. Their strong roots push as they grow. This widens cracks and loosens rock.

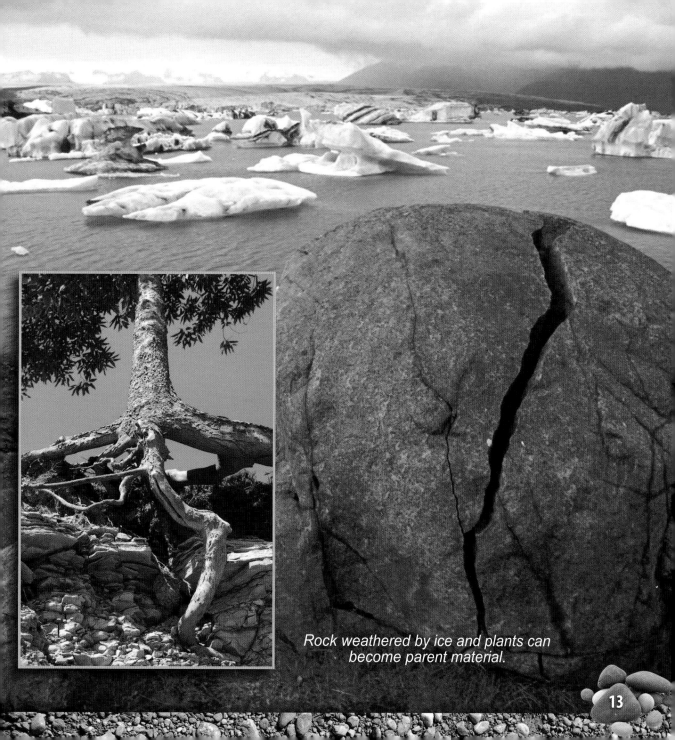

Rock weathered by ice and plants can become parent material.

Getting Carried Away

Weathered rocks don't always stay in place. They may be carried away to new locations by wind, water, and ice. This process is called erosion. It can add to parent material.

The power of moving water is awesome. Rainwater can rush over the land with great force. As it flows toward streams and rivers, it picks up bits of weathered rock.

Ancient glaciers contributed to today's rich soils in places such as Norway.

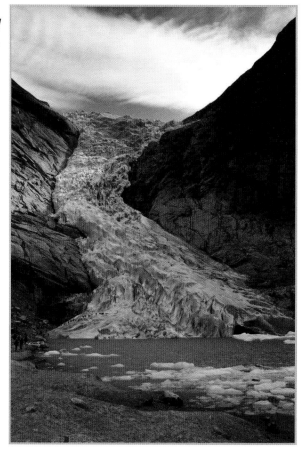

Today, glaciers around the world continue to weather and erode rock.

The moving water carries sand, silt, and clay downstream. These lightweight sediments may be carried all the way to lakes and oceans. But if the water becomes calm, they settle to the bottom.

Rivers and lakes sometimes flood across nearby land. In time, the water returns to its normal depth. But it can leave behind silt, sand, clay, and **organic** matter on land. These materials become part of the soil.

Blowing wind can also pick up tiny particles loosened by **weathering**. When the wind dies down, they are dropped off in new places. Or, they may be left behind when they run into other surface features. Wherever they land, they can become parent material.

Glaciers help soil formation, too. As they scrape along the ground, glaciers weather the rock beneath them. They also carry the rock along. This eroded rock may become parent material.

The Circle of Life

Have you ever left a banana sitting too long on the counter? Has the milk in your refrigerator ever gone sour? Bananas turn spotty, black, and soft. Milk becomes smelly and lumpy. **Organic** materials like these don't change on their own. Bacteria and fungi cause them to decay. These tiny organisms are everywhere, including in soil.

Nearly 1 billion fungi and 500 billion bacteria can crowd into just 2.2 pounds (1 kg) of soil!

Decay may be smelly, but it is an important natural process. Living things store **nutrients**. After plants or animals die, soil organisms break them down. For example, some creatures chew up dead plants. Beetles and

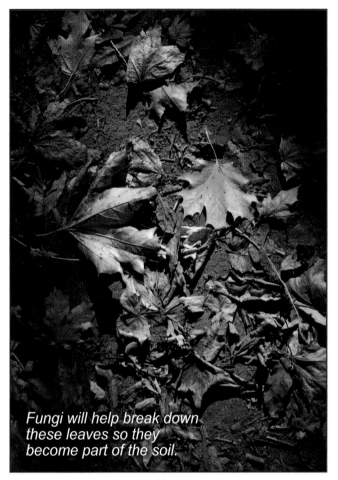
Fungi will help break down these leaves so they become part of the soil.

other insects eat decaying animal remains. This releases the **nutrients** into the soil.

You may recall that decayed plant and animal matter is called humus. This **organic** material is the second main ingredient of soil. It helps the soil support new plants and animals.

Look at the nutrition facts on your breakfast cereal. You'll probably see many of the nutrients that are also found in soil. They include calcium, potassium, and iron. How did those nutrients get into your cereal? They came from soil!

The main ingredient in your cereal is probably wheat, corn, or rice. These plants absorb water, **minerals**, and nutrients through their roots. They use water, air, and sunlight to make food and grow. By eating these foods, you feed your body nutrients.

Land and Climate

You already know about parent material and plants and animals. Land surface features also affect soil development. Picture a mountain with a valley below. Have you ever noticed that high mountains have few trees and plants? The soil is often thinner because soils tend to slip on steep surfaces. This erosion moves the top layer of soil down into valleys. There, thick, rich soils develop where the land is flat.

Climate is important for soil formation, too. It affects **weathering** and plant and animal growth. If an area freezes and thaws often, weathering happens quickly. Lots of rain can also speed up weathering as the water wears down rocks.

If the climate is harsh, the soil will not develop as much. Extreme heat sucks away moisture in soil. Freezing cold slows decay. Many plants do not grow well under extreme conditions. Without enough plants, wind blows away exposed soil.

Cold temperatures slow the decay of organic matter in northern tundra soils.

Soils in tropical climates (left) develop differently from those in arctic areas (right).

A World of Soils

Time is the final factor in soil formation. Soil has a life cycle like people do. It starts out young and then **peaks** in quality. Later, it enters old age.

Parent material, plants and animals, land features, and climate all affect how soil ages. If humus does not have a chance to form, the soil will be less fertile. But under the right conditions, the soil may have time to become deep and well developed.

All five soil forming factors affect what type of

soil develops. Soils occur around the world and change from place to place. There may be many types of soil across a state. In fact, there may be different types of soil in a single field! Scientists have identified more than 20,000 different kinds of soils in the United States alone.

Soils can look very different from one another. They don't all look like the soil in your backyard. Soil can be brown, black, red, or yellow. The color tells scientists about the soil. Dark soil probably contains lots of humus. Red soil may contain lots of iron.

Soil comes in many different colors. What does it look like where you live?

Looking Below the Surface

What does your room look like when it hasn't been cleaned for a while? Chances are, clothes pile up on the floor. Books and papers gather on the desk. You have to dig under one layer to find the next.

Soil also forms layers. Scientists call these layers horizons. They label each one with a letter. Together, soil horizons make up a soil profile.

In some soils, different horizons are well developed and easy to spot.

There are several horizons above the **bedrock**. This is the floor of the soil. This layer is sometimes called the R horizon.

The O horizon is the soil's top layer. It forms at the surface. It is made almost entirely of humus and partly decayed plant and animal matter. The *O* stands for **organic**.

The A horizon is the next layer down. It is a mixture of humus and small bits of **minerals**. Gardeners sometimes call this dark layer topsoil. Plant roots are often in this layer. Just below, the B horizon is full of minerals. It has less humus than topsoil. And, it is lighter in color.

The next layer down is the C horizon. It is made up of broken rocks. Some were **weathered** from the **bedrock** below. Others were eroded from different locations. Rivers or glaciers may have carried them there long ago.

Soil Horizons

O

A

B

C

R

The Best Soil Around

Soils contain different amounts of sand, silt, and clay. The combination of these **mineral** particles determines how soil acts and feels. They affect how water, air, and **nutrients** move through soil.

Sand is the largest of the three particle types. Bits of sand are rough and fairly round. They don't fit together well, so a lot of space is left between them. Water slips right through.

Bits of silt and clay are much smaller than sand. Silt is rounded like sand. But clay is flat and thin like cereal flakes. If you have made pottery, you know clay can be very heavy. Its tiny particles fit together tightly and resist the flow of water. If soil has too much clay, air cannot get in. Then, plants are unable to grow.

Loam is soil with a good balance of sand, silt, and clay. The soil is rich and crumbly. Water can drain well and air can enter between the particles. Plant roots can get the water and nutrients they need to grow. Many plants grow best in loam.

Clay (top left), *loam* (right), *and sand* (bottom left) *soils*

25

Living with Soil

Earthworms, bacteria, and fungi are not the only organisms that live in soil. They share their surroundings with countless other important creatures. Many small animals dig and burrow into soil. This creates space for air, which can aid soil health.

Soil is an important **natural resource**. So, it needs protection from pollution and too much erosion. Pollution affects the health of soil as well as those who depend on it. Too much erosion washes away soil altogether.

Having too little **organic** matter can increase soil erosion. Luckily, many people work hard to prevent this. Ranchers do not let animals eat too much in a single field. When forests are cut down, some material is left behind. This adds to the **organic** parts of soil. Planting certain trees and plants also helps. Their roots help hold soil in place.

COMPOST!

Compost is one way everyone can improve the soil in his or her own backyard. Gather plant parts such as grass clippings and coffee grounds. In a bin, layer them with soil and leave the mixture to decay. After several months, the material will be ready to be added to garden soil. Compost improves soil structure and adds nutrients. So, plants love it!

Standing Strong

Besides being protected, soil must be studied. In 1173, construction began on a splendid new tower in Pisa, Italy. Yet even before it was finished, problems appeared. The beautiful white marble tower began to lean.

Sometimes, buildings fall because of poor construction. But that was not the problem in Pisa. The heavy tower had been built on soil that was soft like jelly! Over the years, it leaned more and more.

Something had to be done to save the tower. In the 1990s, engineers propped it up with cables and weights. Then, they dug out some of the soil to make the tower lean back toward straight. It remains tilted. But for now, the Leaning Tower will not fall.

Modern builders try to prevent such problems by using **soil mechanics**. Before a building goes up, scientists study the soil where it will stand. Each type of soil settles differently under heavy weight. So, engineers design the best **foundation** for each type of soil. This helps buildings last and keeps people safe.

Do you still have that jar of soil? Take it back outside and pour it in a garden. Keep an eye on it, because something may grow in it. That's what soil is all about!

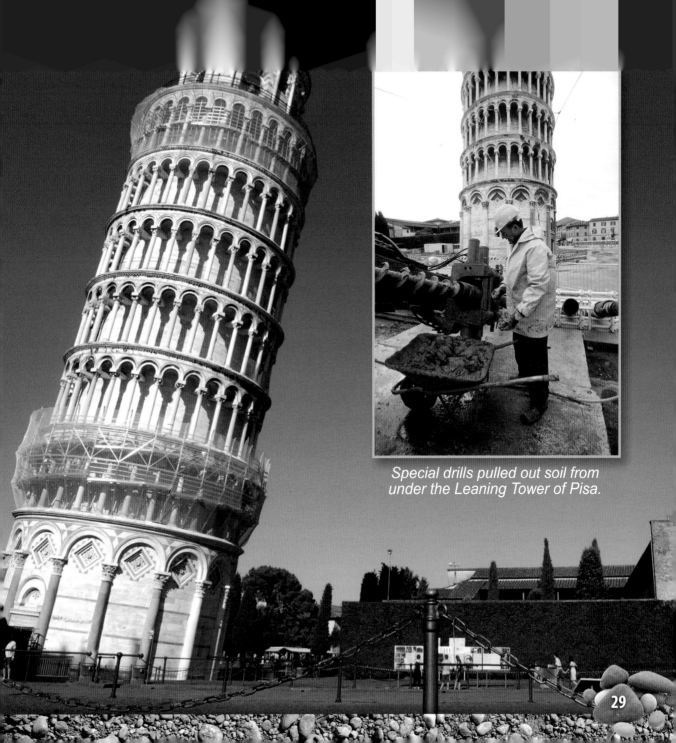

Special drills pulled out soil from
under the Leaning Tower of Pisa.

Glossary

bedrock - the solid rock beneath soil and looser rock.

casting - the waste product of an earthworm.

dissolve - to cause to pass into solution or become liquid.

foundation - the base or support upon which a building rests.

mineral - a nonliving solid with a specific chemical makeup that occurs naturally on Earth.

natural resource - a material found in nature that is useful or necessary to life. Water, forests, and minerals are examples of natural resources.

nutrient - a substance found in food and used in the body to promote growth, maintenance, and repair.

organic - relating to or coming from living things.

peak - to reach the highest point.

soil mechanics - the study of the physical features of soil on which buildings, roads, and other structures may be built.

weathering - the breaking down of rock in its original position at or near Earth's surface. Something that is weathered has experienced weathering.

Saying It

fungi - FUHN-jeye
humus - HYOO-muhs
loam - LOHM
pedologist - pih-DAH-luh-jihst
Pisa - PEE-zuh

Web Sites

To learn more about soils, visit ABDO Publishing Company on the World Wide Web at **www.abdopublishing.com**. Web sites about soils are featured on our Book Links page. These links are routinely monitored and updated to provide the most current information available.

Index

B
bacteria 16, 26

C
clay 15, 24
climate 12, 18, 20
color 21, 23

D
Darwin, Charles 4, 5, 6, 12

E
earthworms 5, 6, 12, 26
England 4, 5
erosion 14, 15, 18, 23, 26

F
fungi 16, 26

G
glaciers 15, 23

H
horizons 22, 23
humus 6, 10, 17, 20, 21, 22, 23

L
land surface features 12, 18, 20
Leaning Tower of Pisa 28
loam 24

M
minerals 6, 10, 12, 17, 23, 24

N
nutrients 16, 17, 24

O
organic matter 6, 15, 16, 17, 22, 26, 27

P
parent material 12, 14, 15, 18, 20
plants and animals 6, 12, 16, 17, 18, 20, 22
pollution 26
protecting soil 26, 27, 28

R
rocks 4, 12, 14, 15, 18, 22, 23

S
sand 15, 24
silt 15, 24
soil formation 10, 12, 14, 15, 18, 20, 21, 22
soil mechanics 28
soil profile 22

T
time 12, 20

U
United States 21

W
weathering 12, 14, 15, 18, 23